# Daughters of Imani
## Young Women's Bible Study

By Tamara Lewis and Richelle B. White

Edited by Marilyn E. Thornton

MANUFACTURED IN THE UNITED STATES OF AMERICA

ISBN 978-0-687-34223-5

Cover Design/Illustration: Keely Moore

05 06 07 08 09 10 11 12 13 14—10 9 8 7 6 5 4 3 2 1

# Table of Contents

# Introduction

Welcome to a Bible study created especially for African American young women! DAUGHTERS OF IMANI: YOUNG WOMEN'S BIBLE STUDY exists to enhance the overall development of Black American girls ages eight to eighteen as they move through adolescence, targeting the emotional and spiritual needs of this population. This curriculum is best used in conjunction with the entire rites-of-passage program but is useful for any girls' youth or study group to help them engage in discussion that will aid in their development as women of faith.

*Imani* is a Swahili (East African) word meaning "faith." This term is used to represent one of the principles of Kwanzaa that stresses the importance of believing in God, in self, and in our communities. We use it here to maintain that becoming a whole person includes gaining a better understanding of one's relationship with God, with oneself, and with one's heritage. In a world that strives to diminish the importance of God by emphasizing materialism, which can destroy one's sense of self through media images, and that often portrays the African American community as one that is not viable (as on the news), Black American Christians need materials that help them deliver a message of hope and love to the younger generation. Women need to be reminded that the God in the Bible is a God of faithfulness and that positive, biblical examples for faithful womanhood can be found and used as role models. Enough of Jezebel and Delilah!

Join us in these eight lessons that feature female children of the most high God. DAUGHTERS OF IMANI will help you engage your students in thought-provoking discussion and spiritual growth. The study is designed to motivate participants to gain greater self-knowledge and is built on the firm foundation of the Word of God. This curriculum gives growing girls and young women a chance to investigate the Bible from a perspective that can help them become daughters of faith.

## To the Bible Study Leader

The *Daughters of Imani* Bible studies consist of eight Bible lessons that focus on personalities and actions in biblical situations featuring women. Each lesson has three sections, or mini-lessons, labeled A, B, and C, each of which can be taught as a stand-alone session. Each section has activities and discussion questions that will help engage students in the learning process. Therefore, this Bible study can be spread over a twenty-four-week period or taught in eight weeks, depending on the time allotted. You can conduct the program in conjunction with the *Daughters of mani Planning Guide: Christian Rites of Passage for African American Girls* in two ways: three mini-lessons a month for an eight-month period, or one lesson (sections A, B, and C) a month for eight months. You can also use this curriculum as an eight-week stand-alone teen Bible study for girls, separate from the *Christian Rites of Passage* program.

Here are some tips for leading this Bible study:

• Pray as you prepare to teach.

• Read all primary and secondary Scripture ahead of time. Make sure that you understand the directions for the suggested activities and that you have the needed supplies. You may choose to create additional questions and activities as well. You may also find other Scriptures that might add to your students' understanding.

• Some of these Bible lessons cover sensitive material for which you may want to do some additional reading. These subjects require the ability to communicate honestly concerning menstruation, endometriosis, the status of women in ancient society, and so on. Remember how important it is for young women to understand their bodies. Be willing to help them understand the world of the Bible stories as it pertains to women.

• Start each session by playing a musical selection of your choosing. The study offers a suggestion for each session, but you may be aware of recordings that are more in tune with the young people of your community. Select something that will engage them and that is appropriate for the lesson material.

• You will need a CD player and appropriate CDs. *Under the Baobab Tree, Volume 2 Contemporary Music CD* is available from Abingdon Press (2004; ISBN 0687007070). Other suggested music can be found on the following CDs: *Welcome to the Village,* by Pastor Kirbyjon Caldwell and the Windsor Village UMC Mass Choir (2002); *This Is Your Life,* by Out of Eden (2002); *Soul Inspiration,* by LeJuene Thompson (2001); *Lifestyle: A Worship Experience,* by The Katinas (2002).

• Find maps of modern-day Africa and the Middle East.

• Have fun with this material! Enjoy your students!

# The Samaritan Woman: Knowing God, Knowing Me, Knowing You

## Get Ready

• If you are doing a mini-lesson, you might begin section A, B, or C of Lesson 1 with the class listening and moving to "Lord, I Want to Know You," by Kirbyjon Caldwell and the Windsor Village UMC Mass Choir *(Welcome to the Village)*. However, the class may prefer some other selection that indicates a need to have a relationship with God.

• Don't forget to pray at the beginning of each session.

## Get Set

• Before Part A of Lesson 1, take turns reading the entire story of the Samaritan woman (**John 4:1-30, 39**):

*¹Now when Jesus learned that the Pharisees had heard, "Jesus is making and baptizing more disciples than John" ²—although it was not Jesus himself but his disciples who baptized — ³he left Judea and started back to Galilee. ⁴But he had to go through Samaria. ⁵So he came to a Samaritan city called Sychar, near the plot of ground that Jacob had given to his son Joseph. ⁶Jacob's well was there, and Jesus, tired out by his journey, was sitting by the well. It was about noon.*

*⁷A Samaritan woman came to draw water, and Jesus said to her, "Give me a drink." ⁸(His disciples had gone to the city to buy food.) ⁹The*

Samaritan woman said to him, "How is it that you, a Jew, ask a drink of me, a woman of Samaria?" (Jews do not share things in common with Samaritans.) [10]Jesus answered her, "If you knew the gift of God, and who it is that is saying to you, 'Give me a drink,' you would have asked him, and he would have given you living water." [11]The woman said to him, "Sir, you have no bucket, and the well is deep. Where do you get that living water? [12]Are you greater than our ancestor Jacob, who gave us the well, and with his sons and his flocks drank from it?" [13]Jesus said to her, "Everyone who drinks of this water will be thirsty again, [14]but those who drink of the water that I will give them will never be thirsty. The water that I will give will become in them a spring of water gushing up to eternal life." [15]The woman said to him, "Sir, give me this water, so that I may never be thirsty or have to keep coming here to draw water."

[16]Jesus said to her, "Go, call your husband, and come back." [17]The woman answered him, I have no husband." Jesus said to her, "You are right in saying, 'I have no husband'; [18]for you have had five husbands, and the one you have now is not your husband. What you have said is true!" [19]The woman said to him, "Sir, I see that you are a prophet. [20]Our ancestors worshipped on this mountain, but you say that the place where people must worship is in Jerusalem." [21]Jesus said to her, "Woman, believe me, the hour is coming when you will worship the Father neither on this mountain nor in Jerusalem. [22]You worship what you do not know; we worship what we know, for salvation is from the Jews. [23]But the hour is coming, and is now here, when the true worshipers will worship the Father in spirit and truth, for the father seeks such as these to worship him. [24]God is spirit, and those who worship him must worship in spirit and truth." [25]The woman said to him, "I know that Messiah is coming" (who is called Christ). "When he comes, he will proclaim all things to us." [26]Jesus said to her, "I am he, the one who is speaking to you."

[27]Just then the disciples came. They were astonished that he was speaking with a woman, but no one said, "What do you want?" or, "Why are you speaking with her?" [28]Then the woman left her water jar and went back to the city. She said to the people, [29]"Come and see a man who told me everything I have ever done! He cannot be the Messiah, can he?" [30]They left the city and were on their way to him....

[39]Many Samaritans from that city believed in him because of the woman's testimony, "He told me everything I had ever done."

# *Part A: Them*
### Bible Focus: **John 4:4-9**

- Have the students re-read **John 4:4-9** from their Bibles.
- Group Discussion: Talk about the prejudices you may have against people who are different from those you hang with. Who are the people you would say are "them"?

## Them

During Jesus' time, Jews typically hated Samaritans and vice versa. Why? To make sense of this conflict, we need to briefly explore this aspect of Israel's history.

After King Solomon's reign, Israel was divided into a northern kingdom called Israel, and a southern kingdom called Judah. Israel's capital city was Samaria, and Judah's capital was Jerusalem. Samaria became so powerful and important that the name became associated with the entire area, whose people were called Samaritans.

Eventually, Israel was conquered by the Assyrians, and Judah by the Babylonians. Hebrew royal families and priests of the people were taken away to live in other lands. Different nations of people were brought in to inhabit the area known as Samaria. These groups mingled with the Israelites who had been left behind, so the resulting new group, called Samaritans, was no longer "purely" Hebrew by race or religion.

When the Judean Hebrews, who had been deported to Babylon, returned to Palestine, they looked down on the Samaritans, calling them racially impure, not real Hebrews, and certainly not Jews. By the time of Jesus, the Jews and the Samaritans hated each other because of racial, ethnic, and religious prejudice. They refused to associate with each other. For this reason, Jews refused to travel through Samaria, although the trek was the most direct route between Galilee and Judea. Even though discriminatory practice was the norm, in our story for today, Jesus chose to travel directly through Samaria and to even talk with a Samaritan woman.

## Debrief

1. Jews and Samaritans did not get along because of racial and religious differences. Discuss how stereotyping a group can hurt the self-esteem of the group's members.
2. If a Jew were to find herself among Samaritans, what do you think would happen? What would happen to a Samaritan among Jews? How would that person feel?
3. Have you ever felt that you were discriminated against or treated with prejudice for being African American, female, or both? Talk about this situation.

**4.** What was radical about Jesus' decision to travel through Samaritan territory? How much more radical was the decision for Jesus to speak with a Samaritan woman? What does this story tell us about the character of Jesus?

## Activity: Bible Search

Since these Scriptures may help the group understand the history between the Jews and the Samaritans, have a race to see who can find read the Scriptures first: **1 Kings 14:19-20, 29-31; 2 Kings 17:1-6, 24-28; 2 Kings 24:10-17, 2 Chronicles 36:22-23.**

## Closing Prayer for a Mini-lesson

Dear God,

Help me to love all of your children. You have created all of the people of the earth. Loving them helps me to love you better. And loving you helps me to love myself. In Jesus' name, Amen.

*Go!*

## Part B: Her
### Bible Focus: **John 4:6-9**

• Have your students read **John 4:6-9** from their Bibles.
• Make up a conversation in which you and your friends are trying to decide whether to talk to a person who is not usually in your group.

## Her

In Part A, we reflected on the issue of prejudice between two groups. As African Americans, we know that this animosity exists between White and Black people. African Americans can hold prejudice against other ethnic groups or against other Black people because of their skin color, hair texture, neighborhood, nationality, or language. So we can relate to how the Jews' and Samaritans' prejudice kept them from getting along. This context helps us understand why Jesus' actions in this story are so special. Jesus was aware of Jewish-Samaritan prejudice, but as a Jew, he chose to walk through Samaria, an area most Jews would never go through.

What about the Samaritan woman? Drawing water was and still is considered women's work in places without indoor plumbing. The task is usually done early in the morning so that people could have water for the day. But verse six reports that the encounter between Jesus and the woman occurred around noon, the hottest time of day. Also, drawing water was a kind of social ritual for women. They would gather around the village's well and talk, laugh, and just spend time together. Clearly, something is strange about the Samaritan woman coming at this odd time.

One suggestion is that she did not have any friends in the village and was not liked by the other women. This suggestion might explain why she came to the well when she knew no one else would be there. She would rather suffer in the heat and draw water alone than face the women of her village. She must have felt lonely and sad.

## Debrief

1. Can you identify with what the Samaritan woman may have been going through?
2. Have you ever felt cut off from the group? What did you do about this situation?
3. What are some of the reasons you or others may have not been liked or accepted in your school, church, or community?
4. How can a person gain high self-esteem when others don't accept him or her?
5. How important is being accepted by other people? Why?

## Activity: Song Search

Back in the day, there was a song called "I'm In With the In Crowd." What are some of the songs playing on the radio now that talk about the "in" crowd, the "homies," or the "kinfolk"? Make up a song or rap that includes everyone in the class.

## Closing Prayer for a Mini-lesson

Dear God,
Thank you for loving me. Thank you for letting me to be in your "in" crowd. Help me to reach out so that no one is left out of the circle of love. In Jesus' name, Amen.

## Go!

## Part C: Him

Bible Focus: **John 4:7-30, 39**

- Have the group read **John 4:7-30, 39** from their Bibles.
- Invite the group to act out the Bible story. You will need someone to represent Jesus, the Samaritan woman, the disciples, and the villagers.

## Him

Let us now examine the conversation that Jesus had with the Samaritan woman. This conversation represents the longest dialogue between Jesus and another person that was recorded in all four Gospels. Jesus talked with her in depth and alone, disregarding the common practice of the time that men should not talk in public with a woman, not even with their wives. This custom is held even now in some places in the Middle East where women must be totally covered in public and separate from men. When the disciples came (verse 27) and found Jesus talking to a woman, they were shocked because that act simply was not done. Jesus, however, did not appear to be concerned about the social practices of the day. His love overruled and overcame racism and sexism.

Jesus opened up the conversation by asking the woman for a drink of water. A person had to bring a vessel to scoop up the water out of the well, but Jesus didn't have one. When Jesus addressed the Samaritan woman, she got an attitude. Jesus did not care about her attitude. He continued the conversation and began to open her eyes, explaining to her that regardless of her situation (which Jesus knew all about) she could experience the true love of God. She could be forgiven and accepted. Jesus reached out to the Samaritan woman, and she was transformed. She lost her attitude and her isolated status at the same time. She ran back to her village to tell her neighbors all about Jesus. In so doing, she brought her whole village to Christ.

## Debrief

**1.** Describe in your own words what happened in the Bible story.
**2.** What is the most significant thing to you about the story?
**3.** How did Jesus help increase the Samaritan woman's self-esteem?
**4.** How does Christ help increase your self-worth and esteem?
**5.** How does your relationship with Christ affect your relationships with other people?

## Activity: Testimony

Take turns telling the rest of the class about a, b, and/or c.
**a.** What this story means to you
**b.** What Christ means to you
**c.** How you hope a relationship with God will affect your life

## Closing Prayer for All of Lesson 1

Dear God,
You are my Creator, and I want to know you. The better I know you, the better I will know myself. Help me to lead others into knowing you. In Jesus' name, Amen.

# The Queen of Sheba: She's a Diva

## Get Ready

• If you are doing a mini-lesson, you might begin sections A, B, and C of Lesson 2 with the class listening and moving to "Now I Sing," by Out of Eden *(This Is Your Life)*. However, the class might prefer some other piece that indicates the joy of knowing who you are in Christ.
• Don't forget to pray at the beginning of each session.

## Get Set

• Before Part A of Lesson 2, take turns reading about the Queen of Sheba (**1 Kings 10: 1-10, 13**):

¹*When the queen of Sheba heard of the fame of Solomon, (fame due to the name of the LORD), she came to test him with hard questions. ²She came to Jerusalem with a very great retinue, with camels bearing spices, and very much gold, and precious stones; and when she came to Solomon, she told him all that was on her mind. ³Solomon answered all her questions; there was nothing hidden from the king that he could not explain to her. ⁴When the queen of Sheba had observed all the wisdom of Solomon, the house that he had built, ⁵the food of his table, the seating of his officials, and the attendance of his servants, their clothing, his valets, and his burnt offerings that he offered at the house of the LORD, there was no more spirit in her.*

⁶*So she said to the king, "The report was true that I heard in my own land of your*

*ccomplishments and of your wisdom, ⁷but I did not believe the reports until I came *nd my own eyes had seen it. Not even half had been told me; your wisdom and *rosperity surpass the report that I had heard. ⁸Happy are your wives! Happy are *hese your servants, who continually attend you and hear your wisdom! ⁹Blessed be *he LORD your God, who has delighted in you and set you on the throne of Israel! *Because the LORD loved Israel forever, he has made you king to execute justice and *ighteousness." ¹⁰Then she gave the king one hundred twenty talents of gold, a great *quantity of spices, and precious stones; never again did spices come in such *quantity as that which the queen of Sheba gave to King Solomon. . . .*

*³Meanwhile King Solomon gave to the queen of Sheba every desire that she *expressed, as well as what he gave her out of Solomon's royal bounty. Then she *returned to her own land, with her servants.*

# Go!

# Part A: Sheba
### Bible Focus: 1 Kings 10:1-2

- Have your students re-read **1 Kings 10:1-2** from their Bibles.
- What do you know about Somalia, Ethiopia, Eritrea, Yemen, and Djibouti? Where can you find information about these places?

## Sheba

This story describes the Queen of Sheba's visit to King Solomon and his court in Jerusalem. Sheba included modern-day Djibouti, Eritrea, Somalia, Ethiopia, and Yemen. Although your social studies book may divide the continent of Africa from the Middle East and Arabia, in ancient times there was no such division. Eastern Africa, the Middle East, and Arabia were zoned as continuous empires and kingdoms in many instances throughout ancient history.

The empire of Sheba had become rich from international trade in spices, precious metals, and stones. When the Bible and other historical records mention Sheba, they describe the kingdom as wealthy and prosperous. Just as Africa is now, the continent was rich in many resources, such as gold, wood, spices, and animals that were in demand all over the world. Because of its location, Sheba could control trade routes coming from all parts of Africa, Arabia, and Asia, and controlling the routes through taxation and trade agreements with other countries gave Sheba a lot of power. The Israelite King Solomon would have wanted to establish positive relations with Sheba to have beneficial trade agreements for Israel.

The Queen of Sheba was responsible for the prosperity, organization, and peace of her nation. When she heard about the riches and splendor of Israel, which was relatively new on the international scene, she may have been doubtful. After all, before David, Israel had been a raggedy band of tribes. She may have also wanted to make sure that Israel was not a threat. Before establishing any agreements between Sheba and Israel, the queen had to see what Israel had to offer. As a thorough administrator, she could not take someone else's word for it. She had to know for herself.

## Debrief
1. Look at maps of modern-day Africa and the Middle East. Make a note of the location of Ethiopia, Eritrea, Somalia, Djibouti, and Yemen.
2. The Queen of Sheba has been portrayed as a beautiful, Black queen covered with jewels. Why is she viewed as an exceptional role model for African American girls?

## Activity: Diva Search
Think of contemporary Black women who are efficient and powerful leaders like the Queen of Sheba, and name them.

## Closing Prayer for a Mini-lesson
O God of the Universe,
Thank you for making me a Black girl. You have made me smart and you have made me beautiful. Help me to be a gracious queen. In Jesus' name, Amen.

*Go!*

## Part B: The Queen
### Bible Focus: 1 Kings 10:3-10

• Have the students re-read **1 Kings 10:3-10** in their Bibles.
• Make a list of questions you would like to ask a knowledgeable person. Now see if someone in the class knows the answers to your questions.

# The Queen

Legends and archaeological accounts round out the historical background on the Queen of Sheba. The *Kebra Nagast* is an ancient book containing religious, folk, and rabbinic traditions of Ethiopians who worshipped the Hebrew God, Yahweh. It tells of a love story between the Queen of Sheba, called Makeda, and King Solomon. There are also several references to a Bilkiqs, Queen of Sheba, in Ancient Yemen.

The Bible tells us that the Queen of Sheba not only had business concerns but also an interest in Solomon's wisdom. The queen had intellectual and spiritual questions for Solomon, whose well-known wisdom was a gift from God. A woman of reflection and insight, the queen looked to Solomon for the answers to her questions.

She wanted to talk to someone whose mind was as sharp as hers, so she tested Solomon with hard questions. One can just imagine how difficult those questions were. Maybe they were about mathematics, astronomy, and science. Some questions were theological. The queen learned about Yahweh, went back to Sheba, and taught her people. (After World War II, when Jews were being returned to Israel from all over the world, Ethiopians whose ancestors had been worshipers of Yahweh since the days of Solomon also came.)

Solomon answered all her questions, displaying his keen intellect. The Queen of Sheba must have been amazed, because she went on to ask him more questions. There was nothing that the king could not explain to her.

People say knowledge equals power. The Queen of Sheba understood that the more knowledge that she had, the more powerful she could be. Being a diva, she did not visit just to get something, even knowledge. She came with something to offer: gold, spices, and precious stones, which she gave to Solomon. She was a powerful woman.

## Debrief

1. What is your impression of the Queen of Sheba?
2. What are some of the things you do to improve your mind?

## Activity: Bible Trivia

Create your own Bible-trivia game.

## Closing Prayer

All-knowing God,
You know that I want to be a diva. Thank you for my mind, my intellect, and my ability to learn. Help me to always be willing to develop these gifts so that I can be a diva for you. In Jesus' name, Amen.

*Go!*

# Part C: The King
### Bible Focus: 1 Kings 10:13

• Have your students re-read **1 Kings 10:13** from their Bibles.
• Now read **Luke 11:31**.

## The King
King Solomon, son of David, was the last king of the unified Israel. He was very impressed with the Queen of Sheba and was interested in every word that came out of her mouth. He wanted to please her in every way, so her wish was his command. Not only did Solomon give the Queen gifts that recognized her as a head of state, which that would go into the treasury of Sheba, increasing its wealth—he gave her personal gifts, which let her know that he was a great king with much stuff. The Queen of Sheba returned to her country greatly enriched, politically and personally.

Her visit with Solomon has been recorded in the histories of her country and in the Bible. Jesus mentioned the queen as an example of the value in seeking wisdom and greatness. He says she "came from the ends of the earth to listen to the wisdom of Solomon" and would rise and condemn those who refused to follow Jesus' ways **(Matthew 12:42b)**. After all, Jesus' wisdom is greater than Solomon's. On their road of faith, girls can model themselves after the Queen of Sheba.

## Debrief
1. The queen must have thought a lot of herself to be able sit down and talk with a person of great wisdom. How would you get ready to talk to an important person?
2. How did Jesus know about the Queen of Sheba, whom he calls Queen of the South?
3. What are some of the ways to gain wisdom?

## Activity: Skit
Act out the story of the Queen of Sheba and Solomon. You may want to dress up.

# Closing Prayer for All of Lesson 2

Dear God,
You knew my ancestors, whether they were in Ethiopia, ancient Ghana, or elsewhere. You are the source of my faith. Give me your wisdom. Help me to follow your Son, Jesus Christ. Amen.

# The Daughters of Zelophehad: Family Unity

## Get Ready

• If you are doing a mini-lesson, you might begin sections A, B, and C of Lesson 3 with the class listening to "Brighter Days," by LeJuene Thompson *(Soul Inspiration)*. However, the class might prefer some other selection that indicates the joy of knowing who you are in Jesus Christ.

• Don't forget to pray at the beginning of each session.

## Get Set

• Before Part A of Lesson 2, take turns reading the entire story of the daughters of Zelophehad in **Numbers 27:1-11:**

*Then the daughters of Zelophehad [zuh-low'-fuh-hahd] came forward. Zelophehad was son of Hepher son of Gilead son of Machir son of Manasseh son of Joseph, a member of the Manassite clans. The names of his daughters were: Mahlah, Noah, Hoglah, Milcah, and Tirzah. ²They stood before Moses, Eleazar the priest, the leaders, and all the congregation, at the entrance of the tent of meeting, and they said, ³"Our father died in the wilderness; he was not among the company of those who gathered themselves against the LORD in the company of Korah, but died for his own sin; and he had no sons. ⁴Why should the name of our father be taken away from his clan because he had no sons? Give to us a possession among our father's brothers."*

*⁵Moses brought their case before the LORD. ⁶And the LORD spoke to Moses, saying: The daughters of Zelophehad are right in what they are saying;*

*you shall indeed let them possess an inheritance among their father's brothers and pass the inheritance of their father on to them.* [8]*You shall also say to the Israelites, "If a man dies, and he has no son, then you shall pass his inheritance on to his daughter.* [9]*If he has no daughter, then you shall give his inheritance to his brothers.* [10]*If he has no brothers, then you shall give his inheritance to his father's brothers.* [11]*And if his father has no brothers, then you shall give his inheritance to the nearest kinsmen of his clan, and he shall possess it. It shall be for the Israelites a statute and ordinance, as the* LORD *commanded Moses."*

## Go!

## Part A: Patriarchy
### Bible Focus: **Numbers 27:1-2**

• Re-read **Numbers 27:1-2** from your Bibles.
• Discuss the make-up of your family. How many sisters, brothers, aunts, uncles, cousins, and play relatives do you have?

## Patriarchy

Moses and the people of Israel had escaped from Egypt and slavery. After many years of wandering in the wilderness, land assignments were finally being made. Most of the people who had originally left Egypt were dead, including Zelophehad of the tribe of Manasseh (son of Joseph). The Hebrews had a patriarchal system that left women dependent on men for sustenance and identity. (Many ethnic groups in Africa and the Middle East continue to follow this system of societal organization.) In a patriarchy, women generally have few rights, and without men they have no rights. All property is passed down through male relatives, and women without men are left with nothing.

The daughters of Zelophehad came together to make a request of Moses. Their names are recorded as Mahlah, Noah, Hoglah, Milcah, and Tirzah. Often, biblical writers did not name women as individuals in their own right. But these women's coming together and standing before Moses gave them a place in biblical history. This fact is the most significant aspect of today's session.

Before the sisters came together to stand before Moses, they must have had to work and plan together as a family to make this decision. In a spirit of unity as sisters, they supported one another and stood for one another. The daughters of Zelophehad demonstrated how women can work together and how a family can advocate for its survival and well-being through unity.

## Debrief

1. Imagine what life was like for the Israelites out in the wilderness, where they lived in tents, traveled from place to place, endured scorching heat, and looked for food and water. What did the land assignments mean for these wanderers?
2. How did this family of women come to agreement? What were some of the things they had to consider? What methods might they have used to overcome disagreements and arguments?
3. A familiar saying is, "The family that prays together stays together." What role does prayer have in the lifestyle of your family?

## Activity: Bible Semantics

Read **Psalm 133.** If you see the word *brothers,* replace it with *sisters;* then read it again and replace the word *brothers* with another word that fits. (The New Revised Standard Version uses the word *kindred.)* What are some other words that fit? *(Church, neighborhood, etc.)*

## Closing Prayer for a Mini-lesson

Dear God,

Thank you for my family and friends. Help me to see all of my sisters as your children. Help me to be willing to work together with others for justice and peace in your world. In Jesus' name, Amen.

*Go!*

## Part B: The Request
### Bible Focus: **Numbers 27:3-4**

- Re-read **Numbers 27:3-4** from their Bibles.
- Review what has happened in the story thus far:
    1. The Israelites were receiving land assignments from Moses.
    2. Five women, whose father Zelophehad (zuh-low' fuh-hahd) had died in the wilderness, came together to make a request of Moses.
    3. Women had no standing in ancient Hebrew society.

# The Request

Mahlah, Noah, Hoglah, Milcah, and Tirzah stood before Moses and all of the people in the congregation, which consisted of the men of Israel. Women presenting themselves to men was a bold act, and going together was a good decision. The daughters wanted the land that had been due to their father.

They told Moses that their father had died in the wilderness and had not been a part of the rebellion led by Korah. (In previous years, Korah had recruited 250 men to challenge Moses and Aaron's leadership. These men felt that they were just as qualified as Moses to lead the people. God put an end to their rebellion by making the earth split apart, swallow the rebels, and then return to normal (**Numbers 16:1-40**). The daughters of Zelophehad assured Moses that their father had had no part in this event but had died a natural death.)

The five daughters were left and no sons, so the inheritance would have typically passed on to the next male heir, perhaps the brother of the deceased. With the land goes the family identity and heritage. If these women did not receive the land, their father's name would be forgotten. Why should the family suffer this loss just because Zelophehad's children were women? The five daughters demanded to have their portion of land.

The daughters of Zelophehad were not only making a claim to receive the inheritance of their father but were also claiming their worth as women in the eyes of the community and in the eyes of God. The daughters were saying that they were valid members of the community. Their womanhood should not impact their value as members of the family and of the community. They belonged to and were part of that family! When the community was not acting in a way that respected their value and status in the family, then these women dared to stand up. This boldness shows their high regard for their father's name, for their heritage, and for community. These women loved their family enough to take a stand.

# Debrief

1. Have you ever had to challenge your family about certain things? If so, discuss some of those things
2. How do people challenge injustice or unfairness in their communities?
3. How do you and your friends handle differences or disputes?

# Activity: Mock Court

Imagine that your circle of girls wants something special from the church body, such as a special day, a special room, or money. How would you get ready to make your request? Who will do the talking, and how? Plan your strategy, and present your request to a large group.

## Closing Prayer

Dear God of Justice,
Thank you for always listening to me. Help me to listen to others with love and a spirit of fairness. Give me the strength to speak boldly for what is right. In Jesus' name, Amen.

*Go!*

## Part C: The Response
### Bible Focus: **Numbers 27:5-11**

- Re-read **Numbers 27:5-11** from your Bibles.
- Have a short time of prayer. Each person may write a prayer request down on a slip of paper and place it in a basket or other container. Each person will pick a prayer slip and briefly pray aloud about the prayer request.

## The Response

In this session, the focus is on the response of God to the request of the daughters of Zelophehad. When Moses heard the request of the daughters, he went directly to God instead of trying to make the decision on his own or to rely on the opinion of the other men. God responded that in this particular situation the daughters of Zelophehad had the right to inherit their father's property. God also told Moses to make a general decree. In this decree, if a man died and had no son, the inheritance would go to his daughter. In this way, God expanded the law to include not just sons but also daughters in the event that there was no son. God made the law broad based on the specific case of the daughters of Zelophehad.

God clearly rewarded the daughters of Zelophehad by supporting their claim and making it a law, giving women greater rights. Although the Israelites of this time lived in a patriarchal system, which greatly limited the rights of women, God was working within the system to improve the lives of women. In this example, we can see how God often works within human society to bring about greater good for all of God's people. By being obedient to God's call for justice and working together as a family of one accord, the daughters of Zelophehad—Mahlah, Noah, Hoglah, Milcah, and Tirzah—are a great example for women to follow.

# Debrief

1. How did Moses handle the request of Zelophehad's daughters? How do you make important decisions?
2. The daughters' demand caused a change in an old and common system: patriarchy. Can you think of another time when people's demands caused a change in the social system?
3. How do laws and practices get changed? Who are the people you would depend on to get justice?

## Activity: Roleplay

Act out the entire story of Zelophehad's daughters. You will need someone to represent the daughters, Moses, the congregation, and God.

## Closing Prayer for All of Lesson 3

Dear God,
You are a God who can make things right. Help me to work in your plan for righteousness and justice. Help me to remember to seek your guidance in everything I do. In Jesus' name, Amen.

# Ruth: Who Is Family?

## Get Ready

- For a mini-lesson, you might begin section A, B, and C of Lesson 4 by playing "Trading My Sorrows," by The Katinas (*Lifestyle: A Worship Experience*). However, the class may prefer another piece indicating that joy is on the way.
- Don't forget to pray at the beginning of each session.

## Get Set

- Before Part A of this lesson, have someone who knows the story of Naomi and Ruth tell it to the class, or have the students read the story.

**Key Points of the Story**

1. Food is scarce in Judah. Naomi moves to Moab with her husband and two sons.
2. Naomi and her husband stay ten years. The sons marry Moabite women.
3. Naomi's husband and sons die. She decides to return to Bethlehem, her hometown in Judah.
4. Naomi releases her daughters-in-law of their obligation to care for her, but Ruth chooses to go to Judah anyway.
5. When they get to Bethlehem, Naomi tells the women of the village to call her Mara (which means "bitter") instead of Naomi ("pleasant").
6. In Judah, Ruth works in the fields to provide food for Naomi and herself. She meets Boaz.
7. Naomi schools Ruth on how to let Boaz know that she is available for marriage.
8. Ruth follows Ruth's instructions, and Boaz goes to court to get Ruth and the property that goes with her.
9. Ruth and Boaz get married and have a baby, who becomes the joy of Naomi's life.
10. The baby, Obed, is the grandfather of David.

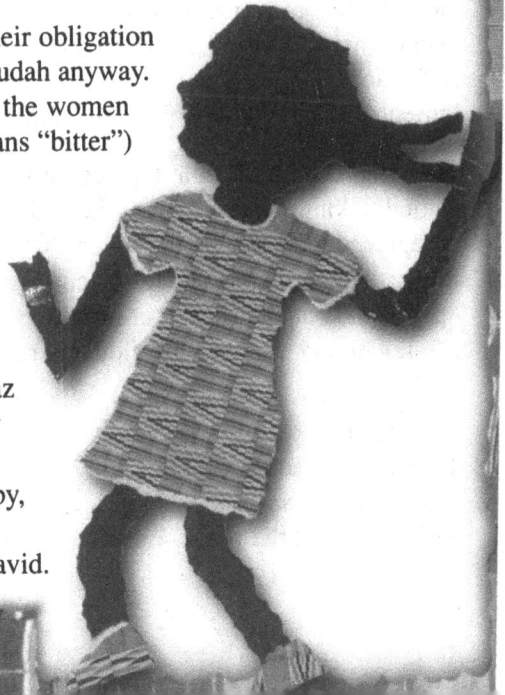

# *Part A: In-laws*
### Bible Focus: **Ruth Chapter 1**

• Using your Bible, read Chapter 1 in the Book of Ruth as a skit.
• You will need a narrator, Naomi, Orpah, Ruth, and women villagers.

## In-laws

Although this story is named after Ruth, it is just as much about Naomi the Hebrew as it is about Ruth the Moabite. The two women were related by marriage. Naomi moved from Bethlehem, her hometown, with her husband and sons to live in Moab because of a famine. When the sons came of age, they got married: one to Orpah, and the other to Ruth. Then all of the men died. Naomi decided to return to Bethlehem.

In a world in which women depended on men for security and status, Naomi and her two daughters-in-law were in a difficult situation. As an older, childless widow, Naomi could expect to lead a poverty-stricken life. The only social security she would have was the care of her daughters-in-law. Even knowing that they were supposed to take care of her, Naomi gave them the chance to stay among their own people.

On their way to Bethlehem, Naomi decided that it was better for them to go back to their homeland. Orpah chose to go back home, but Ruth decided to stay with Naomi. When she had gotten married, she had not only made a pledge to her husband she had also become a part of his family. She honored that commitment by telling Naomi that she would go wherever Naomi went and stay where Naomi stayed. Ruth told Naomi that she would adopt Hebrew ways, worship the Hebrew God, and be buried among Naomi's relatives. Ruth continued the journey with Naomi.

They got to Bethlehem at the beginning of the barley season, and the whole village started talking when they saw them. The women of the village thought that they recognized their home girl, Naomi, who had been gone for at least ten years. When they called her name, she told them to call her something different. Naomi means "pleasant," but she was bitter because she no longer had her husband or her sons. Her life felt empty. She blamed God and renames herself Mara, which means "bitter."

## Debrief

1. Why did Naomi and her family move to Moab in the first place?
2. Look at a map of biblical geography. How far was Moab from the land of Judah
3. Think about the times. What makes the actions of both women unusual?

## Activity: Bible Maps

Look at a Bible map from the days of Judges. Find Bethlehem of Judah. Find Moab. Trace a path that Naomi and her family might have taken from Judah to Moab. How long could it have taken them to walk the distance?

## Closing Prayer for a Mini-lesson

God of Love,
Thank you for sending people who love me. Thank you for giving me people to love. Walk with us as we care for one another in life. In Jesus' name, Amen.

*Go!*

# Part B: Extended Family
### Bible Focus: Ruth Chapters 2–3

- Review key points 6–8.
- Discussion: Many women are interested in learning what to do to "get a man." Magazine articles and TV characters such as Nikki on *The Parkers* are dedicated to this subject. What are your thoughts on this matter? How should a young lady go about "getting a man," or should she?

## Extended Family

Upon arriving in Bethlehem, Ruth and Naomi began to create a life for themselves. The first item on the agenda was food. According to Hebrew custom and law, the poor could gather leftover grain from the harvest after the workers had gone through (**Leviticus 19: 9-10**). This act was called gleaning. Ruth suggested that she glean in the fields so that she and Naomi would have food. Ruth happened to choose a field that belonged to a relative of Naomi's husband. This rich man, called Boaz, noticed Ruth and asked about her. One of his workers told Boaz how kind this Moabite woman had been to her mother-in-law. Boaz told Ruth to remain in his fields. He pulls strings to make things easier for her, instructing his male workers not to harass her and giving her extra grain and bread at lunch. Ruth reports everything to Naomi.

When Boaz, a single, older man, had apparently noticed Ruth, Naomi developed a plan. Instead of waiting to see if Boaz would eventually like Ruth enough to propose marriage, Ruth and Naomi put the ball in his court. A clean, sweet-smelling Ruth went to the threshing floor after Boaz had eaten his full. She then slept at his feet to let him know of her availability. When he awoke, she asked Boaz to consider her for marriage, a request he promised to fulfill. One person was standing in the way, and he planned to take care of the matter. In the morning, Boaz sent Ruth home with plenty of grain. If everything worked out, she would be the wife of a man who could take care of her family.

One of the strengths of the Black American family has been the involvement of grandparents, aunts, uncles, and even people unrelated by blood. In the movie *When We Were Colored,* Cliff was first raised by his great grandfather and then by his mother's aunt. The story of Ruth shows that trusting extended family to help out is an old custom. While Boaz was not related by blood to Naomi, he was somehow related to her husband and still had certain obligations to Naomi as family.

## Debrief
1. What was Ruth's original reason for working in the fields?
2. Describe how Ruth got Boaz's attention. What are some of the techniques a Christian young lady could use? that a Christian young lady should avoid?
3. Talk about how extended family has made a difference in your life.

## Activity: Think About It!
Update the story of Ruth. Maybe Boaz is the CEO of a bank or the president of a university. What kind of behavior would be appropriate for these characters?

## Closing Prayer for a Mini-lesson
Dear God,
Thank you for my play family, my real family, and everyone in my family circle. Thank you for my church family: the teachers, leaders, ministers and everyone who help me to grow spiritually. Thank you for all the people who are interested in helping me to grow into everything you would have me to be. In Jesus' name, Amen

*Go!*

## Part C: Ancestors and Descendants
### Bible Focus: **Ruth Chapter 4**

• Review key points 9 and 10.
• Dictionary Search: What is an ancestor? What is a descendant?

# Ancestors and Descendants

After Boaz promised Ruth he would marry her, he decided to get things in order that day. So he went to the entrance of the village, the place where business was done when judges ruled. Just as soon as he arrived, the person he needed to speak to came up. After a clear explanation, the man who had more responsibility for Naomi and her family decided he did not want another wife. He agreed to let Boaz take charge of Naomi's property and all that went with it, including Naomi and Ruth. Boaz sealed the pact by handing his relative his shoe, a gesture that was like signing a contract. Boaz was now free to marry Ruth. All the people at the village gate celebrated, congratulating Boaz with blessings that mention their ancestors Rachel, Leah, Perez, Tamar and Judah.

Ruth and Boaz married and had a baby boy. Naomi once again had family and no longer felt empty and bitter. The women of the village were happy for her, saying her daughter-in-law was worth "more than seven sons" **(Ruth 4:15b).** The women praised God and predicted wonderful things about the new child. In fact, this boy, named Obed, grew up to be the father of Jesse, who became the father of David, the king who unified the tribes of Israel. Centuries later, Jesus was born in Bethlehem, the hometown of his ancestor Naomi and the adopted hometown of his ancestor Ruth.

In the eyes of the community and in the tradition of the Hebrews, Naomi had become a mother again and a grandmother, and she cared for the baby as if he were her own. Now she had a family with whom to live out her days. When women support one another in faith, there is no end to the blessings that can rain down on all.

## Debrief
1. What does the Book of Ruth teach us about faith, love, and cooperation?
2. What is the role of extended family and community is this story?
3. Why do babies bring joy?

## Activity: Baby Shower
At most baby showers, the mother is "showered" with material things she may need when the baby comes. The women of Bethlehem showered Ruth with verbal blessings. Take a few minutes to write down some blessings you would give to a friend or relative who is having a baby. Take turns reading aloud those blessings. Read with joy!

## Closing Prayer for All of Lesson 4

O God from whom all blessings flow,
Thank you for every blessing. I know I have been blessed to be a blessing. Help me to bring joy to my family, to my community, and to the world. In Jesus' name, Amen.

# The Bleeding Woman: Healing and Wholeness

## Get Ready

• If you are doing a mini-lesson, you might begin sections A, B, and C of Lesson 4 with the class listening to "There's Nothing Too Hard," by Lamar Campbell & Spirit of Praise *(Under the Baobab Tree, Volume 2 Contemporary Music CD).* But the class may prefer some other piece that indicates that God can do anything.
• Don't forget to pray at the beginning of each session.

## Get Set

• Before Part A of Lesson 5, take turns reading the story of the woman who had been bleeding for twelve years, found in **Mark 5:24b-34:**

*[24]A large crowd followed [Jesus] and pressed in on him. [25]Now there was a woman who had been suffering from hemorrhages for twelve years. [26]She had endured much under many physicians, and she had spent all that she had; and she was no better, but rather grew worse. [27]She had heard about Jesus, and came up behind him in the crowd and touched his cloak, [28]for she said, "If I but touch his clothes, I will be made well." [29]Immediately her hemorrhage stopped; and she felt in her body that she was healed of her disease. [30]Immediately aware that power had gone forth from him, Jesus turned about in the crowd and said, "Who touched my clothes?" [31]And his disciples said to him, "You see the crowd pressing in on you; how can you say, 'Who touched me?'" [32]He looked all around to see who had done it. [33]But the woman, knowing what had happened to her, came in fear and trembling, fell down before him, and told him the whole*

*ruth.* <sup>34</sup>He said to her, *"Daughter, your faith has made you well; go in peace, and be healed of your disease."*

## Go!

# Part A: Sick and Broke
### Bible Focus: **Mark 5:24b-26**

• Using your Bible, re-read **Mark 5:24b-26.**
• Talk about the last time you went to the doctor.

## Sick and Broke

This Bible lesson deals with a story within another story, in which Jesus is on his way to help a young girl who is dying **(Mark 5:21-24a).** These two situations indicate the precarious health conditions during the time of Jesus, when the life expectancy was forty years. For women, who were were expected to produce as many children as possible starting at age fourteen, good health was even more elusive. Women were not only expected to rear children and care for their homes and husbands but also to work outside the home. In Jesus' community, people were farmers, raising plants such as wheat and olive trees. Like the young women in Boaz's work force **(Ruth 2:8),** women worked the fields to supply food for their family.

Living in this scientific era, we may have difficulty understanding the significance of a lack of running water, vaccines, and medicine. Such conditions remind us of the problems many communities continue to face. Poor access to healthcare, substandard living conditions, disease, and malnutrition plague a good part of the world. Until 1943, when penicillin became widely available, humanity died of infections easily cured by the drug. Even today, doctors do not have a complete understanding of how the human body works. And whatever help is available costs money. The woman in the story had been bleeding for twelve years. She had spent all she had in search of a cure for her condition. Her doctors had no idea what was causing her illness or how to cure it. She was broke and getting worse.

## Debrief

1. How do you feel about the majority of women in the world, especially women of color, continuing to face some of the same conditions as women did in Jesus' day?
2. What in the story demonstrates the desperation of the people, including the woman?
3. How does access to healthcare (doctors, nurses, medicine) affect the quality of life?

## Activity: Think About It!

How can Christians work to better the quality of life and health for all people? Put your heads together to create a project idea that focuses on community health.

## Closing Prayer for a Mini-lesson

Creator God,

Thank you for allowing me to live in this present age in which good medical help is available. Give me the wisdom to do the things that keep me healthy. Give me compassion for people who are sick and hurting. In Jesus' name, Amen.

## Go!

# Part B: Faith and Action
### Bible Focus: Mark 5:27-30

• Using your Bible, re-read Mark **5:27-30**.
• Briefly discuss: When you know that someone is very sick, what is your reaction?

## Faith and Action

The people in the story are part of the Israelite heritage, which extends back to Moses. According to the Law of Moses, women were considered ritually unclean during their monthly period and for seven days thereafter (**Leviticus 15:19-26**). Because unclean persons were required to remain separate from the mainstream community, a bleeding woman had to stay at home. Although she was allowed to perform certain types of labor during this time, everything she touched would be considered unclean. The Hebrews took these precautions because they thought blood was a spiritual and physical poison that endangered the life and health of anyone or anything with which it came in contact. Blood from a woman was considered doubly unclean.

The woman in our reading was a special case. Her menstrual period had continued for twelve long years. During that time, she could not touch or be touched by anyone without the contact being considered outside the will of God (**Leviticus 15:25-28**). Yet she touched Jesus' outer garment. She had heard about him and believed that she could receive healing without being detected. This way, she would not be accused of trying to contaminate another person. Her risky action paid off. Immediately she felt the change in her body. Her bleeding stopped; she had been healed. But she did not go undetected, because even with a crowd pressing upon him, Jesus was aware of the healing power that had been released from his being.

Most people have experienced rejection. Young girls play cruel games in which one of them is shunned as having "the cooties." Not so long ago, the menstrual period was referred to as "the curse." In a male-oriented society, menstruation may seem abnormal. However, God created women this way. Women should not be considered unclean for simply being women. Jesus accepts women just the way they are.

## Debrief

1. The Hebrews were not the only ones who viewed the female body as physically corrupt because of menstrual blood. Many ancient societies had this view and used it to justify discrimination and oppression of women. Nowadays, some cultures in Asia, Africa, and the Middle East have practices that demonstrate similar views. What are your feelings about menstruation?
2. In contrast to any negative views of the female body, how do you know that your body is sacred and unique?
3. Can you imagine what life was like for ritually unclean persons? Which would be worse: the pain of physical illness, or the emotional pain of exclusion?

## Closing Prayer for a Mini-lesson

O God of Healing,
Pour out your Spirit on those who suffer. Help me to show mercy to all. Allow me to bring a healing touch or a healing word. In Jesus' name, Amen.

*Go!*

## Part C: Reach Out, and Be Healed
### Bible Focus: **Mark 5:31-34**

• Using your Bible, re-read **Mark 5:31-34.**
• Stand in a circle and hold hands with your classmates. Take turns praying for people who are suffering.

## Reach Out and Be Healed

The woman with the bleeding disease was quite bold for being in the crowd. She may have been suffering from a form of endometriosis, or she may have had fibroid tumors in her uterus. (Women of color frequently have these illnesses). Nevertheless, she was "sick and tired of being sick and tired," a phrase coined by Fannie Lou Hamer.* Having been ill so long, she felt she had nothing to lose. Despite the unlawfulness of touching someone, this woman dared to reach out and touch Jesus. powerful faith took over her soul, and she trusted and believed in the power of God. Her faith was so strong and the power of Christ was so real that the instant she touched Jesus' garment, she was healed.

Even Jesus could feel the power of her faith, and he stopped and asked who had touched him. When the woman came forth, he commended and blessed her, calling her "daughter" and showing he had the power to return her into right standing in th community. She was no longer unclean and outcast. Neither was she required to go to the temple to be pronounced clean by the priests like the leper in **Luke 5:12-14.** The Word of Jesus and her faith were enough.

We can identify with the woman with the bleeding disease, since most of us know how rejection feels. We may even have dealt with illness or witnessed the sickness of a loved one. This woman shows us the power of faith. For in the name of Jesus Christ, we can be healed and transformed; all we have to do is reach out.

## Debrief
1. How did the Hebrew rules about menstruation equal a kind of violence against women?
2. What is so remarkable about the woman's actions?
3. How did Jesus treat the woman?

## Activity: Think About It!
Update this story. Maybe the woman is infected with HIV or has AIDS or cancer. What is the response of the Christian community?

## Closing Prayer for All of Lesson 5

Merciful God,
Pour out your mercy on those who are infected with HIV and who suffer from AIDS. Teach me your ways, O Lord, so that I will not become a part of this epidemic. Show me ways to support healing and wholeness in my community. In Jesus' name, Amen.

* "Sick and Tired of Being Sick and Tired: The Politics of Black Women's Health" is also the title of an essay by Angela Y. Davis that can be found in *The Black Women's Health Book: Speaking For Ourselves*, edited by Evely C. White (Seal Press, 2004; ISBN 1878067400).

# Deborah: A Strong Leader

## Get Ready

- If you are doing a mini-lesson, you might begin sections A, B, and C of Lesson 2 with the class listening and moving to "Rise Up," by The Cross Movement *(Under the Baobab Tree, Volume 2 Contemporary Music CD)*. However, the class might prefer some other piece indicating that believers must take a stand for God.
- Don't forget to pray at the beginning of each session.

## Get Set

- Before Part A of Lesson 2, take turns reading the story of the woman who led the battle against the enemies of the Hebrews **(Judges 4:1-10):**

¹*The Israelites again did what was evil in the sight of the LORD, after Ehud died.* ²*So the LORD sold them into the hand of King Jabin of Canaan, who reigned in Hazor; the commander of his army was Sisera, who lived in Harosheth-ha-goiim [huh-roh'-shith-huh-go'-ihm]. ³Then the Israelites cried out to the LORD for help; for he had nine hundred chariots of iron, and had oppressed the Israelites cruelly twenty years.*

⁴*At that time Deborah, a prophetess, wife of Lappidoth [lap'ih-doth], was judging Israel. ⁵She used to sit under the palm of Deborah between Ramah and Bethel in the hill country of Ephraim; and the Israelites came up to her for judgment. ⁶She sent and summoned Barak son of Abinoam from Kedesh in Naphtali [naf' tuh-lie], and said to him, "The LORD, the God of Israel, commands you, 'Go, take position at Mount Tabor, bringing ten thousand from the tribe of Naphtali and the tribe of Zebulun. ⁷I will draw out Sisera, the general of Jabin's army, to meet you by the Wadi Kishon with his chariots and troops; and I will give him into your hand.'" ⁸Barak said to her,*

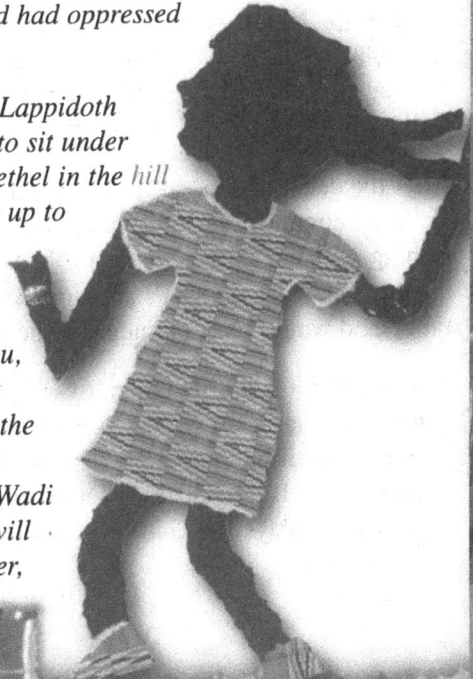

*"If you will go with me, I will go; but if you will not go with me, I will not go."* ⁹*And she said, "I will surely go with you; nevertheless, the road on which you are going will not lead to your glory, for the LORD will sell Sisera into the hand of a woman." Then Deborah got up and went with Barak to Kedesh.* ¹⁰*Barak summoned Zebulun and Naphtali to Kedesh; and ten thousand warriors went up behind him; and Deborah went up with him.*

## Go!

# Part A: Judges
### Bible Focus: Judges 4:1-3

- Re-read **Judges 4:1-3** from your Bibles.
- Name several TV shows that feature real-life judges and courtrooms. Which show is your favorite?

## Judges

Moses was the first leader of the Hebrew people. He led them through the wilderness from Egypt to Canaan, the Promised Land. He was their first prophet, letting them know what God expected of them. Moses would lead the Israelites into battle as they fought their way into the Promised Land. Moses was also the first judge of the Israelites. On certain days during his leadership, he would sit and make decisions for the people from morning until night (**Exodus 18:13**). Moses set the criteria for what a Hebrew leader should be: a person with good decision-making skills who listens to and speaks for God and is not afraid of conflict or even war.

After the death of Moses, Joshua became Israel's leader. Under his leadership, the Hebrews continued to fight for control of Canaan. They had many successes, but the waning of their faith and their disobedience to God over the generations caused them to suffer from attacks and oppression from neighboring groups. From time to time, God would raise up judges to help the people overcome their enemies.

At one point, God turned them over to Jabin, King of Canaan, as punishment. The commander of his army was Sisera, who lived in a place called Harosheth-ha-goiim [huh-roh'-shith-huh-go'-ihm]. The well-equipped Canaanite army led by Sisera oppressed the Hebrew people for twenty years. Finally, the Israelites begged for mercy. They prayed to God for relief from their enemies.

## Debrief
1. What is a judge?
2. What was the cause of Israel's oppression?
3. What is your definition of a good leader?

## Activity: Mock Court
Using either a biblical or TV model, set up a problem that needs a wise decision. Include the entire class. You will need complainants (those who have the problem), witnesses, a judge, and defendants (those against whom the complaint is brought).

## Closing Prayer for a Mini-lesson
O God of Wisdom,
Thank you for hearing all of my prayers. Help me to listen to you always and to say the things that are pleasing to you. In Jesus' name, Amen.

*Go!*

# Part B: Deborah
### Bible Focus: Judges 4:4-7

• Re-read **Judges 4:4-7** in your Bible.
• How does one train for a contest physically, spiritually, mentally, and emotionally

## Deborah
During the time of Jabin and Sisera's oppression of the Hebrews, Deborah served a judge of Israel. She was a prophet who listened to and spoke for God. Deborah live in the hill country of Ephraim. She would sit under a palm tree half-way between the towns of Ramah and Bethel, and people would go up to her for counsel. As a judge, Deborah governed the tribes of Israel, made laws, and resolved internal disputes. (Most judges were tribal leaders whose military victories earned them governing power.) In addition to her spiritual wisdom, Deborah was quite possibly a successful military chief. She had definitely earned the respect of the Israelites.

One day, she sent a message to Barak, son of Abinoam. He lived in Kedesh in Naphtali. Her position as judge gave her the authority to summon him to her so that he could receive a message from God. When he got there, she told him that God wanted him to take a military position on Mount Tabor against the army of Sisera.

He was to take with him troops from the tribes of Naphtali and Zebulun. God was going to make sure that Sisera would be at the Wadi Kishon with his chariots and army. Barak and his troops would start the battle on high ground, while Sisera and his troops would start the battle in a dried creek bed, the low ground. This factor alone would give Israel an advantage. God was going to insure Barak's success, Deborah gave him a God-inspired military strategy.

## Debrief
1. Name the main characters in this story.
2. How do these people relate to one another?
3. What are some things that give you an advantage in life?

## Activity: Artwork
Draw a picture of (a) Deborah under the palm tree with people coming, (b) Deborah prophesying to Barak, or (c) the battle plan arranged by God.

## Closing Prayer for a Mini-lesson
Lord God of All,
Teach me how to share in all of your resources. Help me to know that you can provide abundant life for each one of us. In Jesus' name, Amen.

*Go!*

# Part C: Barak
Bible Focus: **Judges 4:8-10**

• Re-read **Judges 4:8-10** from your Bibles.
• Now read **Luke 11:31.**

## Barak
Barak was a military leader, perhaps a general. He had the ability and authority to call up ten thousand troops from two Hebrew tribes. He no doubt saw the genius of God's plan, which Deborah relayed to him, and knew that God had chosen him to lead the battle. Nevertheless, he lacked the confidence to face Sisera's chariots by himself. So Barak told Deborah that he would go but not without her. He had so much confidence in Deborah that her presence would give him the courage he needed to

get the job done. Deborah let Barak know that she would indeed go. However, the credit he would have gotten for this assured victory would go to someone else. Because of his lack of faith, Barak would not have the privilege of bringing Sisera down. Sisera's demise would come at the hand of another woman (4:17-22).

True to her word, Deborah accompanied Barak back to his hometown, Kedesh, traveling the distance with him up to the hill country. They recruited ten thousand warriors from the tribes of Naphtali and Zebulun. This battle would affect the careers of both Deborah and Barak. The Canaanites had conquered the Israelites' territory and oppressed them for twenty long years. Now God had heard their cries, and Deborah was ready to listen to and speak for God. She was also able to inspire Barak to take leadership to fight this decisive war.

Deborah's story indicates that leaders must be spiritually, mentally, emotionally, and physically ready to lead. Deborah was spiritually ready, because she remained in constant communication with God. Her understanding of what God wanted of her allowed her to communicate to Barak and others God's instructions and wisdom and to inspire Barak to lead the fight against the Canaanites. Deborah was also physically strong. She had the endurance needed to put in long days under a palm tree and the agility needed to walk through the hill country of Israel. She set an example for educators, ministers, and mentors who work to empower others, because she had a direct and positive impact on the well-being of others. This episode in Israel's history shows Deborah to be a great leader who helped create peace in Israel for forty years.

## Debrief
1. How did Deborah show readiness for this contest spiritually, emotionally, mentally, and physically?
2. Have you had teachers who inspired you to do well academically? What were they like, and how did they inspire you?
3. What can you do to become mentally, physically, emotionally, and spiritually strong

## Activity: Inspiration
Create a slogan or poem that inspires a person to do good work.

## Closing Prayer for All of Lesson 6

Dear God,
You are a strong tower. Help me to do the things that will keep me strong in body, mind, and spirit. By keeping myself healthy and strong, I can be more ready to show others to you. In Jesus' name, Amen.

# Esther:
# Positioned for a Purpose

## Get Ready

- If you are doing a mini-lesson, you might begin sections A, B, and C of Lesson 3 with the class listening and moving to "Can't Give Up Now," by Mary Mary *(Thankful)*. However, the class may prefer some other selection that indicates a need to have faith in God and in oneself.
- Don't forget to pray at the beginning of each session.

## Get Set

- Before Part A of Lesson 2, take turns reading the context of the Book of Esther, and **Esther 4:1-17.** Here they are:

**1.** Esther and her cousin Mordecai were Jews in Persia.

**2.** Ahasuerus (uh-has'yoo-er'uhs) was King of Persia, and Vashti was Queen.

**3.** After a seven-day feast with all the male officials and governors, the king commanded an appearance of Queen Vashti so that he could show his guests her beauty.

**4.** Vashti refused.

**5.** The king became so angry that he ordered that her royal position be given to another woman.

**6.** Mordecai, an official at the palace gate, saw the king's royal notice to assemble beautiful young virgins for the King's harem so that the maiden who pleased the king would take the place of Vashti.

**7.** Mordecai took his cousin to be presented before the king, who chose her to replace Vashti.

**8.** When Esther became queen, she kept her Jewishness a secret.

**9.** Haman was also a palace official, ranking above Mordecai. The king had ordered all of the officials to bow down to Haman.

**10.** When Mordecai refused, Haman plotted to have Mordecai and all the Jews in the empire killed.

*¹When Mordecai learned all that had been done, Mordecai tore his clothes and put on sackcloth and ashes, and went through the city, wailing with a loud and bitter cry; ²he went up to the entrance of the king's gate, for no one might enter the king's gate clothed with sackcloth. ³In every province, wherever the king's command and his decree came, there was great mourning among the Jews, with fasting and weeping and lamenting, and most of them lay in sackcloth and ashes.*

*⁴When Esther's maids and her eunuchs came and told her, the queen was deeply distressed; she sent garments to clothe Mordecai, so that he might take off his sackcloth; but he would not accept them. ⁵Then Esther called for Hathach [hay' thack], one of the king's eunuchs, who had been appointed to attend her, and ordered him to go to Mordecai to learn what was happening and why. ⁶Hathach went out to Mordecai in the open square of the city in front of the king's gate, ⁷and Mordecai told him all that happened to him, and the exact sum of money that Haman had promised to pay into the king's treasuries for the destruction of the Jews. ⁸Mordecai also gave him a copy of the written decree issued in Susa for their destruction, that he might show it to Esther, explain it to her, and charge her to go to the king to make supplication to him and entreat him for her people.*

*⁹Hathach went and told Esther what Mordecai had said. ¹⁰Then Esther spoke to Hathach and gave him a message for Mordecai saying, ¹¹"All the king's servants and the people of the king's provinces know that if any man or woman goes to the king inside the inner court without being called, there is but one law—all alike are to be put to death. Only if the king holds out the golden scepter to someone, may that person live. I myself have not been called to come in to the king for thirty days." ¹²When they told Mordecai what Esther had said, ¹³Mordecai told them to reply to Esther, "Do not think that in the king's palace you will escape any more than all the other Jews. ¹⁴For if you keep silence at such a time as this, relief and deliverance will arise for the Jews from another quarter, but you and your father's family will perish. Who knows? Perhaps you have come to royal dignity for just such a time as this." ¹⁵Then Esther said in reply to Mordecai, ¹⁶"Go gather all the Jews to be found in Susa, and hold a fast on my behalf, and neither eat nor drink for three days, night or day. I and my maids will also fast as you do. After that I will go to the king, though it is against the law; and if I perish, I perish." ¹⁷Mordecai then went away and did everything as Esther had ordered him.*

**1.** After the fast, Esther requested an audience with the king. She asked for Haman to join the king and queen for dinner. Haman plans to have Mordecai hanged.

2. Following the banquet, the king is unable to sleep and requests that the book of memorable deeds be brought to him.
3. After reading, he realizes that Mordecai has never been rewarded for saving his life.
4. To Haman's horror, Ahasuerus honors Mordecai.
5. At a second banquet, Queen Esther reveals Haman's evil plot, and the king has him hanged on the gallows Haman had prepared for Mordecai.

*Go!*

# Part A: Mordecai
## Bible Focus: Esther 4:1-5

- Re-read **Esther 4:1-5** from your Bibles.
- Briefly discuss a time when something bad happened in the lives of Africans or Black Americans (such as lynching, the Tuskegee Project, the Rodney King incident, or the Arab attacks on Sudanese tribes) and its effect on our people. How was that happening similar to what the Jews faced in the story of Esther?

## Mordecai

Like the Book of Ruth, the Book of Esther is just as much about another person as it is about the one for whom it is named. In this story, Esther's cousin Mordecai stepped in to raise her when Esther's parents died. He decided to present Esther to King Ahasuerus, advising her to keep her ancestry a secret. With his refusal to bow down and worship Haman, Mordecai angered him. Haman became so angry that he manipulated the king into signing a decree calling for the people to rise up against the Jews throughout Persia. They would even receive money for doing so. When Mordecai discovered the plan, he went through the city of Susa tearing his clothes, mourning bitterly, and wearing sackcloth and ashes. Everywhere the decree was read, Jews behaved like Mordecai, crying and mourning.

Fasting, weeping, and wearing sackcloth and ashes are examples of symbolic prayer. Kneeling or lying on one's face before God represents humility. Outstretched hands represent dependence on God for our needs. Sacrificing represents total dedication and willingness to give up food or something we hold dear (such as chocolate, TV, and hip-hop music) to concentrate before God on a particular need. Weeping shows heart-felt sorrow for a need or crisis. Sackcloth represents a willingness to concentrate not on luxuries and impressing others but on finding God's solution to the problem

...t hand. Ashes placed on the head or face represent a sense of shame, worthlessness, humility, and penitence. Expression of these attitudes is proper when one asks God for help in a desperate communal or individual situation. When one is faced with a problem, praying is the first course of action. That action is what Mordecai did.

## Debrief

1. Describe the way Mordecai prayed.
2. Why is praying in difficult times important? Are difficult times the only times we should pray? Why, or why not?
3. What have African Americans done to express their mourning about negative things that have happened in our history?

## Activity: Conversation Partners

Esther and Mordecai sent messages through a servant. But imagine a one-on-one conversation between Esther and Mordecai. Work with a partner to write the conversation, and read it to the whole group.

## Closing Prayer for a Mini-lesson

Dear God,
Thank you for delivering your people from evil situations. Please help me to remember the struggles of my ancestors so that I may be a better servant, knowing that what they experienced will help me to stand strong and fight for justice. In Jesus' name, Amen.

## Go!

# Part B: Hathach
### Bible Focus: Esther 4:6-14

- Re-read **Esther 4:6-14** from your Bibles.
- Ask: "What are some instances in which God has used African Americans to help save and deliver God's people from evil and destruction?"

## Hathach

Esther's servants saw Mordecai carrying on at the palace gate and reported the matter to Esther. As a woman, Esther could not go out in public, because in ancient society (and in many places in the Middle East now) only men could speak with

men in public. So Esther sent her servant Hathach, a eunuch, to the palace gate to talk with Mordecai and find out what was going on. (Eunuchs were men who guarded women. Their bodies were surgically altered so that they could not have sexual relations with a woman, but they had the strength of a man.)

Mordecai explained things clearly to Hathach and gave him a copy of the king's decree, so that Hathach would give Esther the right message and she would understand the necessity of going to the king. Hathach relayed the message to Esther and delivered her response to Mordecai. Esther was afraid to approach the king without his summons. To do so would mean risking her life. Through Hathach, Mordecai reminded her that her life was already at risk. She was a Jew, and Jews were being targeted. And, Mordecai said, her position in the palace would not protect her from violence. He also told her that perhaps this situation was the reason she was queen.

God leads people to situations where they can be useful to God's purposes. Yet God forces no one to be used, since God can always accomplish God's purposes through someone else. Esther was in such a place when Mordecai challenged her to act in faith and courage to prevent the massacre of their people. She had to decide whether to use her position as queen to bring hope and deliverance for God's people. Black Americans in high positions must also make such decisions. Mary McLeod Bethune, Thurgood Marshall, and Marian Wright Edelman used their positions of authority to help African Americans. Others have chosen to use their positions to ignore or hurt Black people.

## Debrief
1. Why was Esther afraid?
2. How would you have acted in this situation?
3. Have you ever had to do something for the benefit of others and had fears about doing so? If so, what was it, and what was the outcome for those involved?

## Activity: Acrostics

Write an acrostic about courage or leadership. An acrostic is a form of poetry that takes a word and writes a description or action for each letter in the word. The first letter of each line forms the word. For example, an acrostic of the word *God* could be

> Guides my feet
> Offers me grace
> Divine in every way

## Closing Prayer for a Mini-lesson
Dear Lord,
Thank you for choosing me as your child. Grant me knowledge, wisdom, and courage to stand strong in the face of adversity and help others in need. In Jesus' name, Amen.

# Part C: Esther
### Bible Focus: Esther 4:15-17

- Re-read **Esther 4:15-17** from your Bibles.
- Talk about a person you admire who displays both courage and leadership.

## Esther

When faced with Mordecai's challenge, Esther displayed courage and leadership. For the first time, Esther did not receive an order from Mordecai but instead gave him an order, which he obeyed. Esther also determined to take action herself. From this moment on, Esther's relationship with the world changed. No longer was she a passive young girl but a person who took charge. So far in the story, all she had done was to please other people. Now Esther had to appear before the king when he had not called her and convince him to reverse the decree of his highest official.

This desperate situation called for wisdom, cleverness, and solidarity. So Esther told Mordecai to gather the Jewish community for a fast on her behalf. This way, Jews would know that someone was looking out for them and would gain emotional and spiritual strength. Esther and her people had each other's back because Esther was also fasting, along with her maids. For three days, she and the Jewish community fasted, and Esther prepared her heart; then she walked in courage to meet the king.

## Debrief

1. What is fasting, and why is it important?
2. Was Esther's risking her life on behalf of her people necessary?
3. Could the Jews have been saved another way? If so, what way?
4. Is risking one's life for someone or something worth it?

## Activity: Letter Writing

Write a letter to a historical African American who you believe demonstrates courage and leadership. Make sure to tell the person how he or she has influenced your life.

# Closing Prayer for All of Lesson 7

Dear God,
Thank you for your faithfulness in protecting your children. You protect us from dangers seen and unseen. God, help me to be more faithful to you in my Christian journey. Please equip me with boldness and courage in leading your people.

# Phoebe: A Deacon of the Church

## Get Ready

- If you are doing a mini-lesson, you might begin sections A, B, and C of Lesson 2 with the class listening to "Rich," by Brent Jones & the T.P. Mobb (*Under the Baobab Tree, Volume 2 Contemporary Music CD*). However, the class might prefer some other selection that indicates that one's gifts should be used in serving God.
- Don't forget to pray at the beginning of each session.

## Get Set

- Before Part A of Lesson 2, take turns reading about the woman who was a deacon and benefactor of the early church (**Romans 16:1-2**):

*[1]I commend you to our sister Phoebe, a deacon of the church at Cenchreae [sen'kruh-ee], [2]so that you may welcome her in the Lord as is fitting for the saints, and help her in whatever she may require from you, for she has been a benefactor of many and of myself as well.*

# Part A: A Letter

Bible Focus: **Romans 16:1-2**

- Re-read **Romans 16:1-2** from your Bibles.
- Talk about some of your community service activities.

## A Letter

The Book of Romans is a letter from the apostle Paul to Romans Christians during the middle part of the first century A.D. Throughout the letter, Paul lays out what he believes about salvation and faith in Jesus Christ. The letter prepared these Christians for Paul's intended visit to Rome, where he hoped to preach in their house churches and have fellowship with them. In those days, there was no postal service for private citizens. People used messengers or couriers to take letters to others at great distances. Sometimes, if a person happened to be traveling to a certain area, they would be asked to take a letter along and deliver it. The bearer of Paul's letter to the Romans was from Cenchreae, the eastern port of Corinth.

If the letter bearer was unfamiliar to the recipients, an introduction by the writer was necessary. So Paul introduces Phoebe as a deacon of the church at Cenchreae who has carried his letter, giving her a high recommendation. He asks the Romans to welcome her in a manner befitting the saints of God to show hospitality and submission to her, doing whatever she may require.

Paul was able to recommend her because she had proven her worthiness to him, to the community, and to the church. As a deacon, Phoebe had an official position of authority in her church that she had gained by her leadership and service. Her actions had benefited many, including Paul. Phoebe not only knew how to conduct herself in the church among Christians but also knew how to do so in the greater Roman society. She was able to get from one locality to another, operate in the culture in Corinth, and gain enough trust from Paul to appropriately communicate with the people of the Roman church. She had the resources, the strength, and the grace with which to benefit and bless others. Paul clearly had great respect for Phoebe. From this reading, one can see she was a significant leader in the church and had a direct impact on the early Christian movement.

## Debrief

1. What characteristics describe Phoebe?
2. Think about the women leaders in your church and community. How do they demonstrate positive Christian leadership?
3. What are some of the social situations in which Phoebe as a deacon might have found herself? How might she have conducted herself?

## Activity: Roleplaying

Make a list of the various situations in which you find yourself. What are they—going to dinner with parents, having a conference with your teacher, going to the movies with your friends, going out on a date? What are the appropriate ways to conduct oneself in those situations? Discuss your answers in detail. Now choose a scenario and do a roleplay with your classmates.

## Closing Prayer for a Mini-lesson

Giver of All Gifts,

I praise you for my gifts and talents and for making me who I am. Thank you for the opportunities you have given me. Give me the mind to use them to serve you and to serve my fellow human beings. In Jesus' name, Amen.

*Go!*

# Part B: Phoebe
### Bible Focus: Romans 16:1-2

• Re-read **Romans 16:1-2** in your Bible.
• How do you show a person she is welcome? Take turns greeting your classmates.

## Phoebe

Paul wrote his letter to the Romans in Greek. In the letter, he refers to Phoebe as a *diakonos* (die-ah' koe-noes), which means "minister" or "servant." The first deacons were selected by "the whole community of the disciples" to deal with the issue of food distribution among the widows (**Acts 6:2a**). Through their ministry, these servants freed the apostles to concentrate on preaching and praying (**Acts 6:1-6**). Phoebe was a deacon at the church at Cenchreae, which was possibly a church founded by Paul or an offshoot of the church at Corinth. Paul saw her as an effective minister.

n an ancient cemetery in Jerusalem, a tombstone dating back to the fourth century A.D. reads, "The woman deacon Sophia, the second Phoebe." Phoebe lived in the first century, during the time of Paul. Centuries later, she was respected as a role model by other deacons, especially women. Phoebe must have had an enormous impact on the church because she was remembered generations after her death.

Paul advised the Christians in Rome to welcome Phoebe in a manner indicative of their status as saints. A saint is one who has professed Jesus Christ as Savior and who seeks to live a holy life. Paul had certain expectations of them as Christians, such as recognizing this woman as a valuable person and treating her accordingly. They were to treat her with graciousness, as she had been gracious with many others, including Paul.

## Debrief

1. How do you expect to be treated when you visit others in their home?
2. What have been some of your experiences when you have visited other churches?
3. Is there a difference in the meaning of *servant, minister,* and *deacon?* How have you seen these words interpreted?

## Activity: Artwork

Using construction paper, scissors, and glue, create a simple collage that shows the many works of service that women do in your church and community.

## Closing Prayer for a Mini-lesson

Jesus, Lover of my Soul,
You have welcomed me into your kingdom. Give me a welcoming spirit. Teach me to be kind and gracious to everyone I see. In Jesus' name, Amen.

*Go!*

# Part C: Cenchreae
### Bible Focus: **Romans 16:1-2**

• Re-read **Romans 16:1-2** from your Bibles.
• Show the artwork you created in Part B of this lesson.

# Cenchreae

In Paul's reference to Phoebe in Romans, he says she served in the "church at Cenchreae" (**Romans 16:1b**). One other Biblical reference to Cenchreae exists. **Acts 18:18b** says, "at Cenchreae [Paul] had his hair cut, for he was under a vow."

Cenchreae was a suburb of the city of Corinth, a trading and administrative center the area. The suburb was located six miles from the center of Corinth at the easter seaport of the city. This port allowed for the transportation of goods to other place in the Roman Empire. Phoebe may have been used to traveling between Cenchrea and Rome, taking care of business, enlarging her territory, and helping the church

A person of means, she had her own stuff and was able to bless the church with th stuff. As a woman, she would have had to observe the highest decorum as well as exhibit the keenest business sense, because in the Greco-Roman world, women wo regarded as "the weaker sex" (**1 Peter 3:7**).

As Phoebe influenced the church in her leadership role, spiritual leaders can influence young women today. Those who are able to develop a strong faith, good leadership skills, and mature vision usually have dedicated and devoted ministers and other role models. It is important to seek out those persons who exhibit a positive attitude, great faith, and caring spirit. Look for these persons in your fam church, and community. Many of them may be aching to reach out to you to share the good news, give a helping hand, or simply be an ear.

## Debrief

1. How do the lives of Phoebe and women such as Madame C.J. Walker and Mag Lena Walker relate to one another?
2. Phoebe used her influence in a positive way. What are some ways you have see persons use influence, especially financial influence, in positive or negative way
3. How do you handle money? Do you know how to stick to a budget?

## Activity: Write It Down

Make a list of how you have spent your money this week. Write down all expense How much did you save? How much did you give to the church?

## Closing Prayer for All of Lesson 8

Dear God from whom all blessing flow,
The earth and everything in it belongs to you. I want to be a good steward of the material blessings you have given to me. Help me to be obedient to you in the wa spend money. In Jesus' name, Amen.

www.ingramcontent.com/pod-product-compliance
Lightning Source LLC
Chambersburg PA
CBHW010921040426
42445CB00017B/1944